WHAT'S WRONG WITH THE AMERICAN DEMOCRATIC SYSTEM

NICK V. SMITH

About the Author

The author holds a postgraduate degree in Information and Knowledge Administration and has a background in social and humanities studies. With expertise in writing high-quality academic essays, research briefs, and literature reviews, the author focuses on political and institutional issues. He specializes in transforming complex academic concepts into clear, accessible, and publication-ready content.

Table of Content

Introduction

This book presents a current analysis of the functioning of the democratic system in the United States, examining its political structure and its failures.

The American system of democracy has long been regarded as one of the best in the world and has even served as a model for other countries. Established in the U.S. Constitution of 1787 by the nation's Founding Fathers, the system was crafted with a clear democratic structure. The Constitution was written to secure rights and benefits for all Americans.

However, after more than 250 years under this system, the current government has begun to remove and restrict some of the most important civil rights for Americans. These include freedom of expression, the right to protest, access to information, and the freedom to travel within the nation, among others.

This work explores the reasons behind these changes and seeks to identify what is failing in the American democratic system today. What is wrong with it?

The American Constitution

Characteristics of American Constitutions

The American constitutions, especially the Federal Constitution, and to a large degree those of Latin America, which are modeled upon that of the United States, possess certain features that distinguish them from the constitutions of Europe and Asia.

In the first place, they are largely instruments of grants and prohibitions of power, not merely bodies of fundamental law for the organization of government. They are characterized by the detail with which they define and enumerate the powers of the executive, the legislature, and the courts, and by the same detail with which they impose express limitations and prohibitions upon the powers of public authorities, especially the legislature.

These limitations and prohibitions are found not only in the text proper of the Constitution itself but also in elaborate "bills of rights," which precede the formal text. In the federal Constitution, they are found in the first ten amendments. The effect is to create two distinct domains or spheres: one of liberty, within which the individual is allowed freedom of action, and another of authority, within which the government is free to act, subject to restrictions.

Thus, as Burgess remarks, the American constitutions are instruments not only of government but also of liberty. One of their distinctive merits is that they ensure protection for the minority against the possible tyranny and oppression of the majority.

Some of the recently adopted constitutions of Europe, with their elaborate bills of rights, approximate in this respect the American type. However, there is one important difference between them and the American constitutions. In the United States, the sphere of individual liberty created and delimited by the Constitution is protected against invasion or encroachment by the government by being placed under the guardianship of the judiciary, whereas in Europe, it is not.

As is well known, if the legislature, the executive, or any local authority in the United States violates any prohibition or restriction set by the Constitution, the individual who suffers injury as a consequence may appeal to the courts and have the unconstitutional act declared null and void.

In this way, constitutional prohibitions are enforceable through judicial process. The government is kept strictly within the sphere marked out for it by the Constitution. The legislature is not the judge of its own powers. The Constitution is distinctly what it purports to be, namely the supreme law of the state, paramount in authority and superior in dignity and validity to all other law.

In other countries where the Constitution is not placed under the guardianship of the courts, it cannot truly be considered the supreme law. In the last analysis, it stands on a footing of equality with ordinary statutory law and has only such binding force as the legislature chooses to recognize.

Americans naturally believe that their solution to this problem is the only one by which the supremacy of the Constitution over ordinary legislation can be assured and by which individual liberty, as defined and guaranteed by the Constitution, can be safeguarded.

Role of the Constitution as the Protector of Liberty

It should not be concluded, however, that liberty cannot and does not exist in countries whose constitutions contain no bills of rights or formal prohibitions on legislative power, or where, if they do, the judiciary is not empowered to enforce them.

Professor John W. Burgess, in his book *The Reconciliation of Government with Liberty* (1915), maintains that most constitutions outside the United States are defective for this reason. American constitutions explicitly limit government power and place enforcement in the hands of the judiciary, unlike many European systems where legislatures are supreme.

How Does Judicial Review Protect Liberty in the United States?

Courts can declare laws unconstitutional, ensuring that the government remains within constitutional limits.

Is Presidential or Legislative Supremacy Compatible with Constitutional Liberty?

The American model rejects legislative or presidential supremacy, arguing that liberty is safest when the Constitution overrides ordinary law.

In plain English, this means that there is no such thing as constitutional government without a series of constitutional limitations upon its powers, imposed by the sovereign nation on behalf of individual liberty.

Federalism: The United States Constitution has a federal character, as it incorporates the principles of federalism by dividing governmental powers between the central government and the federating units (the states).

The Constitution also incorporates other federal principles, such as separation of powers and checks and balances.

Separation of Powers: The powers of the three branches of government in the United States are distinctly stated and provided for in Article I, Article II, and Article III of the Constitution, covering the Legislature, Executive, and Judiciary, respectively. Therefore, separation of powers is a fundamental feature of the United States Constitution.

Fundamental Human Rights: The U.S. Constitution upholds the tenets of human rights by providing for the basic rights of its citizens, including the right to freedom of speech, association, expression, privacy, liberty, religion, equal protection, property, non-discrimination, and the right to life.

Freedom of Association: The United States Constitution guarantees the right to freedom of association, including the right of citizens to choose their religious beliefs and avoid discrimination on the grounds of religion. The Constitution further establishes the United States as a secular state based on equality of all religions.

Representative Democracy: Democracy is a system of government by the whole population through elected representatives. The U.S. Constitution upholds this tenet of representative democracy by providing for the right of citizens to vote and be elected, hold periodic elections, and join political parties.

Checks and Balances: Checks and balances are a major feature of the United States Constitution. This doctrine ensures equilibrium in the discharge of governmental functions among the various branches of government and prevents arbitrary rule and abuse of power.

Protection of Individual Rights: The Constitution includes explicit limitations on government power to protect personal freedom. The Bill of Rights (the first ten amendments) guarantees liberties such as free speech, due process, and religious freedom.

Limited Government: The Constitution grants specific powers to the government and prohibits others. This creates a balance between a functioning government and the protection of liberty.

Republican Form of Government: Citizens elect representatives who make decisions on their behalf. This system balances popular sovereignty with stable governance.

Compromise Between Large and Small States

The Great Compromise created a bicameral Congress:

- House of Representatives: based on population
- Senate: equal representation (two per state)

The Ten Amendments Explained

The first ten amendments to the Constitution were ratified on December 15, 1791.

First Amendment – Fundamental Freedoms

Protects:

- Freedom of speech
- Freedom of religion

- Freedom of the press
- The right to assemble
- The right to petition the government

Second Amendment – Right to Bear Arms

- Protects the right to keep and bear arms.

Third Amendment – Quartering of Soldiers

- The government cannot force citizens to house soldiers in peacetime.

Fourth Amendment – Search and Seizure

- Protects against unreasonable searches and seizures.
- Requires warrants based on probable cause.

Fifth Amendment – Rights of the Accused

Includes:

- Protection against self-incrimination
- Protection against double jeopardy
- The right to due process
- Rules for eminent domain

Sixth Amendment – Fair Trial Rights

Guarantees:

- A speedy and public trial
- An impartial jury
- The right to counsel
- The right to confront witnesses

Seventh Amendment – Civil Trials

- The right to a jury trial in certain civil cases.

Eighth Amendment – Punishment Limits

- Prohibits cruel and unusual punishment

- Prohibits excessive bail or fines

Ninth Amendment – Unenumerated Rights

- States that people have other rights not explicitly listed in the Constitution.

Tenth Amendment – States' Rights

- Powers not delegated to the federal government are reserved to the states or to the people.

Why the Bill of Rights Matters

The Bill of Rights plays an essential role in American society by safeguarding individual liberties and limiting the powers of the government. It serves as a fundamental protection against government overreach, ensuring that citizens retain key personal freedoms. These amendments guarantee fair treatment for all individuals within the justice system, establishing rights such as due process and trial by jury.

Furthermore, the Bill of Rights helps maintain a balance between federal authority and the rights of states and individuals. By reserving powers not explicitly granted to the federal government, it affirms the principle of federalism and upholds the autonomy of states and the people. Ultimately, the Bill of Rights remains a cornerstone of American democracy, providing a lasting framework that supports freedom, justice, and equality.

American Society

From 1940 to the present, American society has undergone major economic, social, and demographic transformations shaped by war, technological change, and evolving political institutions. During World War II and the postwar era, the United States emerged as a global superpower, experienced rapid industrial growth, and expanded a middle class supported by manufacturing, suburbanization, and government programs such as the GI Bill, though these benefits were unevenly distributed along racial and gender lines.

The mid-20th century saw significant social change through the civil rights movement, expanded women's participation in the workforce, and increased federal involvement in social welfare. From the 1970s onward, economic restructuring shifted employment from manufacturing to services and technology, contributing to globalization, rising income inequality, and regional disparities.

Immigration increased following policy changes in the late 20th century, making the population more ethnically and culturally diverse. In recent decades, advances in digital technology, changes in family structure, and growing political polarization have reshaped public life, while debates over the role of government, social equality, and national identity continue to influence American society within a democratic and market-based system.

Levels of political knowledge in the United States are strongly correlated with educational attainment. Individuals with higher levels of formal education tend to demonstrate greater familiarity with political institutions, policy processes, and comparative political systems. Civic education in primary and secondary schooling varies widely by state and district, often emphasizing national history and constitutional structure over applied political analysis or international comparison. As a result, political understanding across the population is uneven rather than uniformly distributed.

Socioeconomic status influences political engagement and political literacy through access to resources, time, and institutional exposure. Higher-income and professional groups are more likely to participate in political activities, follow policy debates, and engage with governance beyond elections. Lower-income groups often face structural constraints, such as job insecurity, limited time, and reduced access to political networks, that can affect the depth and consistency of political participation. These differences reflect variations in opportunity rather than differences in interest or capacity.

Media consumption patterns play a central role in shaping political awareness. Traditional news sources, academic publications, and long-form journalism tend to provide greater institutional and policy context, while cable news, social media platforms, and algorithm-driven content often prioritize immediacy, personalization, and emotionally salient topics. The fragmentation of media environments allows individuals to select information sources that reinforce existing perspectives, contributing to varied levels of exposure to political complexity across the population.

However, in American society, the value of truth is formally recognized as important, particularly within its legal, journalistic, and educational institutions. Foundational principles such as freedom of speech, a free press, and due process are premised on the idea that truth can be pursued through open inquiry, evidence, personal reflection, and debate rather than imposed by authority.

At the same time, the decentralized media system, strong protections for opinion and expression, and adversarial political culture allow multiple, competing claims to coexist in the public sphere, including those based on ideology, identity, or belief rather than verifiable evidence.

As a result, American society places a high institutional value on truth as a principle, while everyday political and social discourse often reflects ongoing tension between empirical standards, personal conviction, and strategic communication.

Political understanding in American society is best described as unevenly distributed rather than collectively underdeveloped. Differences in education, socioeconomic position, and media exposure shape how individuals encounter, interpret, and engage with political information. These patterns reflect institutional structures and information environments rather than inherent characteristics of the population.

A Hybrid Society

American society in the 21st century is neither fully conservative nor fully liberal; instead, it is a hybrid society with strong liberal trends in culture and strong conservative currents in politics and identity. The balance shifts depending on the issue, the region, and the generation.

How American Society Leans Today

Culturally: More Liberal

Most social attitudes in the United States have moved in a liberal direction since the early 2000s. There is greater acceptance of LGBTQ+ rights, same-sex marriage, and gender equality. Support for racial equality and multiculturalism has also increased. Younger generations, such as Millennials and Gen Z, overwhelmingly hold progressive views on social issues, and urban and coastal regions tend to be strongly liberal.

These trends reflect the influence of modern liberalism, which emphasizes civil liberties, social equality, and government action to address inequality.

Politically: Deeply Polarized

The United States is politically divided between a liberal Democratic Party, shaped by modern social liberalism, and a conservative Republican Party, shaped by traditional values, limited government, and cultural conservatism. Since the 1970s, the parties have sorted ideologically: Democrats have become mostly liberal, and Republicans mostly conservative.

Economically: Mixed

American society supports both free markets and entrepreneurship, which are traditionally conservative traits, as well as government programs such as Social Security, Medicare, and public education, which are associated with liberal policy. This creates a mixed economy in which neither ideology dominates completely.

Regionally: Patchwork

The United States is not ideologically uniform. The coasts and major cities tend to be liberal, while rural areas and much of the South are more conservative. Suburbs often swing between the two. This regional divide is one of the strongest in the country.

Despite liberal cultural shifts, many Americans continue to hold strong religious identities, traditional family values, and skepticism toward government power. These are classic conservative traits that remain influential.

So… Is the U.S. Conservative or Liberal?

It is both.

It is a culturally liberal, politically polarized, economically mixed, and regionally divided society.

It is not a single ideological society but a space in which two powerful traditions, modern liberalism and modern conservatism, coexist and compete for influence.

Ideological polarization in 21st-century America affects constitutional rights not by rewriting the Constitution itself, but by shaping how those rights are interpreted, expanded, restricted, or unevenly applied across states and institutions.

How Diversity Affects Constitutional Rights in 21st-Century America

The result is a country in which the lived experience of constitutional rights varies dramatically depending on political ideology, geography, and the balance of power between conservative and liberal actors.

Conservatives and liberals increasingly disagree not on whether rights exist, but on what those rights mean.

Conservative-leaning interpretations emphasize:

- Originalism (interpreting the Constitution as it was understood at the time of writing)
- Strong protections for gun ownership (Second Amendment)
- Broad religious liberty, including exemptions from certain laws
- Limits on federal power and a preference for states' rights

Liberal-leaning interpretations emphasize:

- A "living Constitution" that evolves with society
- Expanded civil rights protections (LGBTQ+ rights, racial equality, gender equality)
- Strong separation of church and state
- Federal guarantees of voting rights and equal protection

The same constitutional text can produce different legal realities depending on which ideology dominates courts, legislatures, or state governments. Polarization has created what some describe as a "patchwork Constitution," in which rights differ sharply by state. Americans no longer experience constitutional rights uniformly. In many cases, a person's ZIP code influences the scope of their rights.

Courts as Battlegrounds for Ideological Control

Polarization has intensified battles over Supreme Court appointments, federal judgeships, and state supreme courts. Constitutional rights can shift depending on which ideological bloc controls the judiciary.

Research suggests that elite polarization, especially among political leaders, drives institutional conflict and shapes how rights are interpreted.

At the same time, Americans increasingly distrust government, courts, and the media. This distrust is fueled by misperceptions and emotional hostility between parties. People are less likely to believe their rights will be protected fairly. Citizens often interpret legal decisions through partisan lenses, and compliance with constitutional norms weakens.

When trust collapses, rights become more vulnerable to manipulation or selective enforcement.

Political Violence and Threats to Democratic Norms

Emotional polarization, rather than ideological disagreement, drives hostility and increases tolerance for anti-democratic behavior among some groups.

Threats to election workers undermine voting rights. Intimidation affects freedom of expression and assembly. Political violence pressures institutions and weakens the rule of law. When people fear retaliation or instability, rights become harder to exercise.

Rights Become Identity Markers Instead of Shared Principles

Polarization turns constitutional rights into symbols of group identity. For example, guns are often associated with conservative identity, while reproductive rights are associated with liberal identity.

The consequence is that rights are defended selectively rather than universally. This weakens the idea of a shared constitutional culture.

If one characteristic stands out above all others as the most defining feature of American society, it is its extraordinary cultural diversity.

American society is built on multiple cultures, ethnicities, and religions living within the same national framework. A long history of immigration from every region of the world has created a population unlike any other in its composition. This diversity shapes the most important aspects of American society: politics and ideology, social norms and values, public debates about rights, equality, and identity, and even art, music, food, and language.

Diversity is both:

- A source of strength, innovation, creativity, global influence, and pluralism.
- A source of tension, polarization, and debates over immigration, race, identity, and rights.

In other words, diversity is the engine behind both the best and the most challenging aspects of American life.

In the 21st century, the United States is a country in which diversity is both a tremendous asset and a constant source of friction. That duality is part of what makes the nation so complex.

The coexistence of different cultures leads to an ever-evolving set of social expectations and moral standards. Public debates about rights, equality, and identity reflect this dynamic. Diversity fuels passionate discussions about whose rights should be prioritized and how equality and identity are defined.

The blending of traditions enriches American culture, creating a vibrant tapestry of artistic expression and daily life in music, food, language, and the arts.

The Dual Nature of Diversity in the 21st Century

Diversity does not merely influence American society; it structures its politics, its social cohesion, and even how constitutional rights are interpreted and applied. Diversity remains both a tremendous asset and a constant source of friction.

How Diversity Shapes American Politics, Social Cohesion, and Constitutional Rights

In politics, diversity fuels both representation and polarization. American political life is deeply shaped by the country's demographic and cultural variety.

Effects on Political Behavior

Different groups prioritize different rights and policies, creating distinct political coalitions. Urban versus rural divides reflect cultural differences as much as geography. Immigration, race, gender, and religion become central political battlegrounds because they symbolize broader identity conflicts.

Effects on Institutions

Political parties increasingly appeal to identity-based constituencies rather than broad national audiences. Diversity pushes institutions to expand representation, leading to more women, minorities, and immigrants in Congress. At the same time, it can trigger backlash from groups who feel culturally displaced.

The Paradox

Diversity expands democratic participation, yet it can also intensify polarization because groups interpret national identity differently.

The United States is one of the most diverse societies in modern history. That diversity brings both benefits and challenges.

Diversity strengthens innovation and creativity. Cultural exchange produces global influence in music, food, art, and technology. Diverse communities often demonstrate adaptability and resilience.

At the same time, diversity can contribute to fragmentation if shared norms are not continually negotiated. The Constitution is the same document for everyone, yet diversity ensures that it is not experienced in the same way across communities.

Representation Expands, but Consensus Shrinks

As the population becomes more diverse, democratic participation broadens. More women, immigrants, and racial and ethnic minorities run for office. Political agendas increasingly reflect the priorities of groups once excluded from power. New coalitions form around issues such as immigration, policing, reproductive rights, and religious freedom.

This expansion of representation can strengthen democracy by increasing accountability and legitimacy.

However, consensus becomes more difficult. Diversity means more perspectives, but also more disagreement about what the country should represent. Groups interpret "freedom," "equality," and "justice" differently. Political parties increasingly become identity-based rather than policy-based, and elections can transform into cultural battles rather than debates over governance.

The future of democracy depends on whether institutions can manage pluralism without collapsing into permanent gridlock.

Social Trust and Institutional Adaptation

Diverse societies can thrive, but only when institutions actively build bridges. If institutions invest in inclusive education, fair policing, equitable economic opportunity, and civic engagement, diversity can become a source of resilience rather than fragmentation.

The future of democracy hinges on whether the United States chooses to build those bridges or allows divisions to deepen.

The Question of National Identity

For more than 250 years, Americans have debated what "America" means.

On one side is a pluralistic vision in which identity is fluid and inclusive, and the nation is defined by shared democratic values rather than ethnicity or religion. On the other side are competing ideas that can produce division among different parts of society.

The future of democracy depends on whether the country can articulate a national identity that includes everyone, respects differences, and still provides a sense of unity. If it can, diversity will strengthen democracy.

Diversity is not a threat to American democracy; it is the test of American democracy.

American Democratic System

The contemporary American democratic system is characterized by strong constitutional continuity alongside increasing institutional strain. Core democratic mechanisms, including regular elections, separation of powers, judicial review, and civil liberties protections, remain in place and function at the national and subnational levels.

At the same time, structural features such as the two-party system, the Electoral College, and legislative veto points limit representational responsiveness and amplify partisan polarization. Political competition is highly adversarial, with declining trust in institutions, contested narratives about electoral legitimacy, and uneven participation across demographic groups.

Media fragmentation and campaign finance dynamics further shape political behavior and public perception. Overall, American democracy continues to operate within its constitutional framework but faces challenges related to governance efficiency, political cohesion, and public confidence.

The American democratic system faces challenges that stem primarily from its institutional design and contemporary political conditions (polarization), rather than the absence of democratic mechanisms.

Representation is uneven due to features such as the Electoral College, malapportioned legislative bodies, and district-based elections, which can produce outcomes that diverge from aggregate voter preferences. Governance efficiency is constrained by separation of powers and multiple veto points, making policy change slow and increasing the likelihood of stalemate.

Political polarization has intensified within a two-party system that limits ideological sorting and encourages zero-sum competition. Campaign finance structures amplify the influence of organized and well-resourced actors, affecting perceptions of political equality. Media fragmentation and algorithm-driven information environments complicate shared factual understanding, while declining trust in institutions weakens democratic legitimacy.

Together, these issues do not indicate democratic failure but reflect accumulated structural tensions within a system designed for stability rather than rapid adaptation.

American democracy is under strain due to polarization, weakened institutional guardrails, money-driven politics, and declining public trust. These issues reinforce each other and create a system that struggles to solve problems, govern effectively, or maintain public confidence.

Polarization is the most widely cited threat to U.S. democracy. Eighty-one percent of Americans believe democracy is threatened (The Leadership Conference on Civil and Human Rights, 2025), largely because the country is deeply divided. Experts describe polarization as the "drifting apart" of ideologies to the point where compromise becomes nearly impossible. For that reason, citizens view opponents as enemies rather than fellow Americans, resulting in an inability to pass major reforms, gridlock in Congress, and hostility between parties.

Research highlights cracks in three essential pillars of democracy:

- Protecting elections
- Defending the rule of law
- Fighting corruption

These pillars are facing "serious threats," according to the *Democracy Playbook 2025*, due to the erosion of trust in election outcomes, increased political interference in legal processes, and greater vulnerability to corruption.

Money and Special Interests Dominate Politics

According to the Pew Research Center, 85% of Americans say campaign costs make it hard for good people to run for office; 84% say lobbyists and special interests have too much influence. This causes elected officials to prioritize donors over voters, ordinary citizens to feel powerless, and policy outcomes to skew toward wealthy interests.

Dysfunctional Political Institutions

Americans overwhelmingly believe that Congress is more focused on fighting than solving problems (86%). It is difficult to find unbiased political information (68%). Political leaders rarely face consequences for unethical behavior (only 22% think they do).

Misinformation and a Distorted Media Landscape

Experts identify misinformation as a major threat to democracy because citizens cannot agree on basic facts, conspiracy theories spread rapidly, trust in institutions collapses, and elections become battlegrounds of disinformation (it is happening now).

Racial and Economic Inequality

Racial and economic inequality are structural threats to democracy. They produce unequal political representation, barriers to voting, disparities in political power, and social unrest and distrust.

For these reasons, when asked to name strengths of the political system, more than half of Americans say "nothing" or give no answer. This reflects a deep crisis of confidence, lower civic participation, increased support for anti-system candidates, and the weakening of democratic norms.

In Summary: What's Wrong?

The American democratic system is strained by:

- Extreme polarization
- Weakening democratic institutions
- Money-driven politics
- Misinformation
- Inequality
- Public distrust

The United States Government Is Not a Business

The United States government is not a business. It is a public institution designed to operate according to the laws established by the Constitution, with the fundamental purpose of ensuring the welfare of the population through its democratic institutions.

Historically, the founders of the United States explicitly rejected the idea of an economically driven government. They came from colonial experiences where the British Crown acted like an extractive enterprise, imposing taxes without representation. That is why they designed a system based on the separation of powers and popular sovereignty.

The United States maintains a clear separation between government and business activity. The state regulates, manages, and guarantees rights but does not compete in the market.

The Legislative Branch, composed of the House of Representatives and the Senate, is responsible for creating laws that protect fundamental freedoms, such as freedom of speech, freedom of assembly, and the right to decent working conditions.

The Judicial Branch, made up of the Supreme Court and federal courts, is responsible for interpreting and applying the law in disputes between citizens, businesses, or institutions. Its actions are strictly limited to the legal framework, without consideration of political interests.

The Executive Branch, headed by the President, manages public resources derived from taxes. Its role is to enforce the laws and coordinate federal agencies through a cabinet of specialized secretaries.

All these institutions are funded by the taxes paid by citizens to provide essential services such as health, education, infrastructure, and security, thereby contributing to the population's quality of life.

Unlike a company, where resources, including human ones, are exploited to the limit to obtain as much profit as possible, the government does not seek profit. Its "profit" is social welfare: hospitals, schools, roads, safety, and justice. All of this is financed by the taxes paid by citizens.

So why do some people say that the government is a business? Mainly because of the size of the federal budget and the influence of large corporations in politics. But that does not change its nature: the government exists to serve, not to sell.

The U.S. institutional design was created precisely to prevent the government from becoming a business or serving private interests. Its role is to protect rights, manage public resources, and ensure the general welfare of the population.

The Electoral College

The Electoral College has clear advantages and clear drawbacks. Americans remain deeply divided about it. What I can do is lay out the strongest evidence-based arguments on both sides, grounded in reputable sources, so you can evaluate the system on its merits.

How the Electoral College Shapes American Democracy

The Electoral College was created as a constitutional compromise balancing large and small states, concerns about direct democracy, and the structure of federalism. It has remained controversial from the founding era to the present.

Advantages

Supporters argue that the Electoral College:

- Protects the influence of smaller states, preventing a handful of large metropolitan areas from dominating presidential elections.
- Keeps elections decentralized, with states administering their own processes rather than a single national system. This reduces the risk of nationwide recounts or disputes.

- Encourages candidates to campaign across diverse regions, rather than focusing only on population centers.

Disadvantages

Critics argue that the Electoral College:

- Can award the presidency to a candidate who loses the national popular vote, as happened in 2000 and 2016.
- Gives disproportionate power to swing states, sidelining voters in reliably "red" or "blue" states.
- Amplifies the political influence of less populous states, making some votes effectively count more than others.

Public Opinion

Public attitudes reflect this divide:

- About 80% of Democrats favor replacing the Electoral College with a national popular vote.
- Republicans are more split: 53% want to keep it, while 46% prefer replacing it.

What Does This Mean for the Country's Future?

The Electoral College shapes how campaigns are run, how coalitions are built, and how Americans perceive the legitimacy of elections. Because it is embedded in the Constitution, changing it would require a constitutional amendment, a politically difficult process requiring broad national consensus.

Demographic change is one of the most powerful forces reshaping how the Electoral College works, and it is doing so in ways that make the system more volatile, more unequal in representation, and more politically consequential than at any point in modern history. Let us walk through the key dynamics so you can see the full picture.

Population Shifts Change Which States Gain or Lose Power

The Electoral College is tied to the census. As populations move, states gain or lose electoral votes. That means demographic change literally reallocates political power.

States Gaining Influence: Fast-growing, diverse states like Texas, Florida, Arizona, Georgia, and North Carolina have gained seats over the last several decades. These states attract immigrants, young families, and internal migrants from other states.

States Losing Influence: Older, slower-growing states in the Midwest and Northeast, including Illinois, Michigan, Ohio, Pennsylvania, and New York, have lost electoral votes. These states tend to have aging populations and lower immigration rates.

The result is a shifting map where political power follows demographic dynamism.

Diversity Transforms Swing States

The most important political effect of demographic change is that it reshapes which states are competitive.

Examples: Arizona and Georgia, once reliably conservative, became competitive as Latino, Black, and younger voters grew in number. Nevada and Colorado shifted from swing states to leaning more consistently Democratic due to demographic diversification.

Florida became more complex: Latino communities there have diverse political identities, making the state unpredictable.

The Electoral College amplifies these shifts because a small change in population composition can flip an entire state's electoral votes.

The "winner-take-all" rule magnifies demographic trends.

In 48 states, the candidate who wins the popular vote in that state, even by a tiny margin, gets all the electoral votes. This means a demographic group that grows from 20% to 25% can change the entire state outcome. Small shifts in turnout among young, immigrant, or minority voters can swing presidential elections.

Demographic change becomes politically explosive because the Electoral College turns gradual population trends into sudden political shocks.

Urbanization vs. rural decline creates structural imbalance. The U.S. population is increasingly concentrated in large metropolitan areas. But the Electoral College gives disproportionate weight to smaller, rural states.

Consequences: Diverse, urban states like California, New York, and Illinois have less electoral power per voter. Less diverse, rural states like Wyoming, North Dakota, and Montana have more electoral power per voter. This imbalance grows as demographic change accelerates, creating tension between the popular vote, which reflects national demographic reality, and the Electoral College, which reflects state-based representation.

The Electoral College becomes less aligned with the national electorate as demographic change accelerates. The gap between the national popular vote and the Electoral College outcome becomes more likely.

This does not mean the system is "broken," but it does mean the Electoral College increasingly reflects geography rather than population. Demographic change makes the system more contested, and legitimacy debates intensify when outcomes diverge from the popular vote.

Demographic change does not just influence the Electoral College; it reshapes the entire logic of presidential elections. It determines which states matter, which voters are courted, and how political coalitions evolve.

The Electoral College

The Electoral College is the system the United States uses to elect the president, and it works very differently from a simple national popular vote. Understanding it clearly helps explain why campaigns focus on certain states, why some votes carry more weight than others, and why a candidate can win the presidency without winning the most votes nationwide.

The Electoral College is a state-based voting system created by the U.S. Constitution. Instead of voting directly for president, Americans vote for electors who then cast the official votes for president and vice president.

There are 538 electors in total.

A candidate needs 270 electoral votes to win the presidency.

How Electoral Votes Are Distributed

Each state gets a number of electors equal to:

- Its number of House representatives (based on population)
- Plus 2 senators

Examples:

- California: 55 electors
- Texas: 40 electors
- Illinois: 19 electors
- Wyoming: 3 electors

Washington, D.C., also gets 3 electors.

Because of the Electoral College, most states use a winner-take-all system, which means the candidate who wins the popular vote in the state gets all its electoral votes. Even if the margin is tiny (like 0.1%), the winner gets 100% of the state's electors.

Only Maine and Nebraska use a proportional, district-based system.

This winner-take-all rule is what creates swing states, because flipping a state flips all its electoral votes.

The Electoral College does not just influence swing-state strategy; it creates it. Because almost every state uses a winner-take-all system, campaigns do not try to win the country; they try to win the right states. That single design choice shapes every modern presidential campaign.

Campaigns focus almost entirely on a tiny set of states.

In a popular national vote system, every vote would matter equally. In the Electoral College, only the states that could realistically flip matter.

Meanwhile, voters in safe states, such as California, Texas, New York, and Alabama, receive little attention because their outcomes are predictable.

The Electoral College turns a national election into a state-by-state chess match.

Swing states shape the national agenda. Candidates craft messages specifically for the demographics and interests of swing states.

Examples of how this plays out:

- Midwestern swing states push candidates to emphasize manufacturing, trade, and agriculture.
- Sun Belt swing states elevate issues like immigration, suburban growth, and Latino outreach.
- Florida, with its older population and diverse Latino communities, influences debates on Social Security, Cuba policy, and Medicare.

The national agenda becomes a reflection of the priorities of a handful of states, not the entire country.

Campaigns build coalitions tailored to swing-state demographics.

Because winning a swing state yields all its electoral votes, campaigns design strategies around the specific groups that can tip those states.

This leads to intense micro-targeting of suburban voters, heavy investment in turnout operations for Black, Latino, and young voters in states where they are decisive, and messaging crafted for specific cultural or economic concerns unique to each swing state. The Electoral College makes campaigns hyper-strategic and hyper-localized.

Turnout strategy becomes more important than persuasion because the Electoral College rewards campaigns that can surgically increase turnout in key counties rather than appeal broadly across the nation.

A few counties can decide the presidency.

Because swing states are often decided by razor-thin margins, campaigns focus on specific counties that historically tip the balance, like Maricopa County (AZ), Fulton County (GA), Milwaukee County (WI), Miami-Dade County (FL), or the Philadelphia suburbs (PA). For this reason, the Electoral College turns these counties into national battlegrounds, even though they represent a small fraction of the U.S. population.

The map can change as demographics shift. As states become more diverse or more suburban, they can move into or out of swing-state status. Recent examples include Georgia and Arizona, which became competitive as their populations diversified. Colorado and Virginia moved out of swing-state status as demographic trends solidified.

Texas is watched closely because of rapid demographic change.

The Electoral College makes demographic trends politically explosive because flipping a single state can change the entire election outcome.

The Electoral College has a profound and often controversial impact on American democracy because it changes who has political power, whose votes matter most, and how presidents are chosen. Its effects are structural, not accidental; the system itself shapes democratic outcomes.

It creates unequal representation in a democracy. The ideal is "one person, one vote." The Electoral College breaks that principle because small states have more electoral power per voter than large states.

This unequal weighting means the presidency does not reflect the national popular will as directly as in other democracies.

It allows presidents to win without winning the popular vote. This has happened multiple times in U.S. history, including in the 21st century.

A democracy where the majority can lose the presidency faces long-term stability challenges. It turns a national election into a battle for a few swing states. Because of winner-take-all rules, candidates focus almost entirely on states that could flip.

Millions of Americans in "safe states" are effectively ignored, and campaign promises are tailored to the interests of a handful of states. National policy becomes distorted by swing-state priorities.

The democratic impact is that the system narrows political attention to a small slice of the electorate, weakening the idea of equal citizenship.

Meanwhile, it dilutes the influence of large cities, younger voters, diverse states, and immigrant communities.

It reinforces the two-party system. Because you must win states, not votes, the Electoral College makes it nearly impossible for third parties to gain traction. A system that structurally favors two parties can struggle to represent a complex, diverse society.

Supporters argue that the Electoral College protects federalism, prevents regional domination, forces candidates to build broad coalitions, and avoids nationwide recount chaos.

The Electoral College affects democracy by distorting representation, shaping campaign strategy, amplifying geographic divides, reducing the influence of millions of voters, and allowing minority-vote presidents.

It is not simply a voting system; it is a power allocation system that determines who counts, how much they count, and which voices shape the presidency.

The Electoral College has clear advantages and clear drawbacks; Americans remain deeply divided about it. What I can do is lay out the strongest evidence-based arguments on both sides, grounded in reputable sources, so you can evaluate the system on its merits.

Critics argue that the Electoral College can award the presidency to a candidate who loses the national popular vote, as happened in 2000 and 2016; gives disproportionate power to swing states, sidelining voters in reliably "red" or "blue" states; and amplifies the political influence of less populous states, making some votes effectively count more than others.

That is why about 80% of Democrats favor replacing the Electoral College with a national popular vote, while Republicans are more split: 53% want to keep it, and 46% prefer replacing it (2026 Encyclopedia Britannica).

Democratic Political Party

The Democratic Party is one of the two major political parties in the United States. It is generally positioned center-left to left on the U.S. political spectrum. The party emphasizes a larger role for government in managing the economy, regulating markets, and providing social services.

The Democratic Party believes that government can and should reduce economic inequality, provide a social safety net, and regulate businesses to protect consumers, workers, and the environment. In foreign policy, Democrats are more supportive of multilateralism and international alliances. The party tends to prioritize institutional stability, the rule of law, and administrative expertise.

Democrats support progressive or graduated taxation, government investment in infrastructure, education, healthcare, and clean energy, as well as labor unions and worker protections. Their approach to markets is mixed: they accept capitalism but seek to regulate it, oppose monopolies, and support antitrust enforcement. There are internal divides within the party, with moderates favoring incremental reform and progressives pushing for structural changes such as Medicare for All and wealth taxes.

The Democratic Party places a strong emphasis on civil rights and anti-discrimination laws, gender equality, LGBTQ+ rights, and reproductive rights. The party generally supports legal abortion access, expanded voting access, and immigration reform with a pathway to legal status. Policy is often framed in terms of equity and inclusion.

Democrats favor alliances such as NATO and partnerships in Asia and prioritize diplomacy over unilateral action. The party is more cautious about large-scale military interventions than in the early 2000s, though it is not pacifist. Democrats support military aid to allies and U.S. global leadership through institutions.

The Democratic coalition is diverse and includes urban voters, racial and ethnic minorities, younger voters, college-educated voters, labor union members, and a growing share of suburban voters. This diversity creates internal ideological tensions but also gives the party a broad geographic reach.

The Democratic Party has a strong presence in major cities, coastal states, and higher-education hubs. It has a competitive advantage in popular vote totals, fundraising from small donors and institutions, and voter turnout operations in dense population areas.

Major factions within the party include moderates or centrists who emphasize electability and incremental reform, progressives who emphasize structural reform and redistribution, and identity-focused activists who emphasize social justice and representation. The party functions as a coalition of interest groups rather than a tightly unified ideological movement.

(Descriptive, Not Endorsement) Common criticisms of the Democratic Party include that its messaging can appear technocratic or elitist and that it has difficulty translating policy complexity into simple narratives. Internal disagreements can slow decision-making, and the party is sometimes perceived as disconnected from rural or working-class voters without college degrees.

Objectively, the Democratic Party is a broad, coalition-based party that is center-left in policy orientation and institutionally focused. It is strong on policy detail and governance but weaker on emotional or populist messaging.

When analyzing the adaptation of the Democratic Party to the 21st century, we can point out that it still has work to do; however, due to its policies of openness, inclusion, and forward-thinking, its platform is more suited to the needs of modern American society.

In this way, it seeks to protect people's fundamental rights by fostering a productive environment and reducing inequality and racism. It supports humanitarian policies and comprehensive reforms, with strong backing for climate policies, clean energy, and environmental regulation.

The Republican Party (GOP)

Both major political parties in the United States have struggled to keep up with the rapid evolution of American society, which is immersed in an accelerated dynamic in multiple aspects.

However, it is the Republican Party (GOP) that has faced the most obstacles in reaching American society. There is a clear disconnect between the GOP and the majority of American society, as reflected in the legislative action that banned abortion in 2024. This law was widely rejected by women and by much of society, generating expressions such as "my body, my choice." By persisting in enforcing this law, the GOP was punished by voters at the polls.

This episode shows that, in designing and implementing the abortion ban law, the GOP was out of step with the current times, which led American society to consider the measure unacceptable.

The GOP and Its Difficulty Adapting

Through the anti-abortion law, the Republican Party aims for American women to have more children, with the intention of gaining demographic benefits. However, by not understanding the current reality, its actions become outdated and unworkable. This highlights its difficulty in designing and implementing laws suitable for the times, limiting the achievement of its political and economic goals.

Inability to Propose Alternatives to Healthcare

Regarding the Obamacare program, the GOP has also failed to design or implement a system that provides low-cost medical coverage to most of American society. Although this is a basic and priority need, the GOP's only response has been excessive criticism of the Obamacare medical program. However, it continues to be applied because it is a program that meets the current needs of society in terms of healthcare.

Has the GOP Struggled to Adapt to Modern Times?

Many analysts, scholars, and political observers argue that yes, the Republican Party has faced significant challenges in adjusting to the social, cultural, and demographic changes in the United States in the 21st century and in meeting social needs. However, the GOP has chosen to represent and govern in favor of a specific sector of the country, leaving the rest of the country aside.

Demographic Changes Are Advancing Faster Than the Party

The United States has changed profoundly in recent decades: greater racial and ethnic diversity, growth of immigrant communities, an increase in young voters with different values, and expansion of progressive urban and suburban areas. Many analysts say that the GOP has struggled to connect with these emerging groups, especially young people, Latinos, African Americans, urban voters, and college-educated professionals.

This does not mean that it lacks support in these sectors, but that its main base remains more homogeneous and older.

American society has changed in areas such as civil rights, cultural diversity, gender equality, same-sex marriage, and immigration. Many studies point out that the GOP has taken more conservative positions regarding these changes, creating tensions with younger or more progressive sectors of the country.

Internal Ideological Reorientation

The Republican Party has experienced ongoing internal debates and conflicts regarding its ideological direction. These tensions arise as the party confronts the challenge of adapting to modern social and demographic changes while maintaining its traditional conservative principles. As American society evolves, the GOP faces the difficult task of reconciling differing viewpoints within its ranks, which range from maintaining established values to considering new approaches that address current realities.

Electoral Results Reflecting These Tensions

The results of recent elections have highlighted the impact of these internal ideological differences. Electoral outcomes often reveal divisions within the party, as various factions compete to shape its future direction. The struggle between upholding conservative identity and responding to shifting societal needs is frequently mirrored in voter behavior and election performance, making it clear that internal reorientation is both necessary and challenging for the GOP.

Their electoral strategy is based on mobilizing their base, not necessarily on transforming to address the needs of the entire 21st-century American society. Many studies and analyses agree that the GOP has faced difficulties in aligning with certain social and demographic changes of the 21st century, which creates tensions with emerging sectors of American society.

However, it is also true that the party has chosen another form of adaptation, focused on reinforcing its conservative identity and its connection with a specific segment of the country. Since 1980, the

GOP's electoral base has shifted from being a broad conservative coalition (suburbs, businesspeople, religious groups) to a base more concentrated in Southern and Western states, with a strong presence in rural areas, white voters without a college degree, and regions that have gained electoral weight due to population growth.

Changes in the Electoral Map (1980–2024)

The electoral map shows growth of Republican power in the South and West, regions that have gained electoral votes due to population growth, and loss of influence in states in the Northeast and Midwest, which have lost population and electoral votes.

Can the GOP Adapt to Modern Times Without Losing Its Conservative Identity?

This is a difficult question for the GOP because it touches on a real dilemma within the Republican Party: how to modernize without ceasing to be conservative?

It is not an impossible contradiction, but it is a delicate balance. Many analysts agree that it is possible, although it requires deep strategic decisions.

The Republican Party is one of the two major political parties in the United States, generally associated with center-right to right-wing positions. It advocates for a market-oriented economy with limited government intervention, lower taxes, and reduced regulation.

The party typically supports a strong national defense, enforcement of immigration laws, and a federal system that emphasizes states' rights. On social issues, Republicans often promote traditional values and religious freedom, though policy views vary across the party's coalition.

Republican positions are shaped by a broad range of ideological currents, including economic conservatism, social conservatism, and populist nationalism, within the framework of the U.S. political system.

Major Political Challenges Attributed to the GOP

Demographic Shifts

The Republican Party has encountered difficulties adapting to an increasingly diverse, younger, and urban electorate. Reliance on an older, predominantly white rural voter base has become less sustainable as demographic trends shift. Limited engagement with Latino, Asian American, and younger voters has negatively impacted national election outcomes.

Significance: Achieving nationwide success requires broader appeal beyond core supporters.

Social Policy Positions

Firm positions on social issues such as abortion, LGBTQ+ rights, and women's health have contributed to the alienation of moderate and independent voters. The overturning of *Roe v. Wade* and subsequent support for restrictive abortion legislation have been unpopular in several swing states.

Political Implication: It may reduce competitiveness in swing states.

Association with Donald Trump

While former President Trump galvanized the party's base, his influence led to the loss of suburban voters, mainstreamed election denialism, and associated the party with frequent controversy. The challenge of balancing loyalty to Trump supporters with a need for broader appeal has resulted in internal division.

Result: The party faces strategic uncertainty regarding its future direction.

Election Denial and January 6 Repercussions

Endorsing or tolerating unfounded claims regarding the 2020 election outcome has eroded trust among moderates and independents. The events of January 6, 2021, continue to affect the party's reputation.

Strategic Concern: Undermining confidence in the electoral process can be detrimental to long-term governance aspirations.

Policy Communication Limitations

The GOP frequently emphasizes opposition to Democratic policies rather than presenting comprehensive alternative proposals. On issues such as healthcare, infrastructure, climate, and education, critique often outweighs constructive policy solutions.

Voter Perception: There is a lack of clarity regarding the party's positive policy agenda.

Loss of Suburban and College-Educated Voters

Suburban voters, particularly women and college-educated individuals, have increasingly shifted toward the Democratic Party, influenced by rhetoric, cultural debates, and recent political dynamics.

Consequence: Winning competitive states becomes more difficult without broad suburban support.

Internal Divisions

Ongoing conflicts between establishment figures and populist elements within the party have weakened candidate recruitment, messaging, and fundraising efforts. Primaries that elevate more ideologically extreme candidates pose challenges in general elections.

Recurring Issue: Success in primary contests does not guarantee national victory.

Underutilization of Mail-In and Early Voting

Opposition to mail-in voting, especially during the COVID-19 pandemic, decreased GOP turnout in close races. While Democrats adjusted strategies, Republicans were slower to adapt.

Irony: It affects its own base with this measure.

Important Considerations

It is important to note that the GOP has achieved considerable success at the state level, particularly in judicial appointments and legislative control. The party remains nationally competitive and often surpasses expectations. Many perceived missteps are trade-offs that strengthen the party's base but limit broader electoral reach.

Trump Era (2016–2020)

Key Challenges

Leadership Identity

During this period, the Republican Party became strongly associated with President Trump's personal style and conduct, overshadowing traditional conservative principles and resulting in a less distinct party identity.

Decline in Suburban Support

Support waned among suburban voters, especially women and college-educated individuals, which contributed to notable electoral defeats.

Governance and Public Perception

Despite notable policy achievements such as tax cuts and judicial nominations, ongoing administration controversies and inconsistent messaging diminished public trust.

Electoral Outcomes

Although the GOP won the 2016 presidential election by narrow margins in critical states, subsequent years saw losses, including control of the House in 2018, the presidency in 2020, and later the Senate.

Post-Trump Era (2021–Present)

Election Denialism

Support for election denial narratives has posed significant obstacles to attracting independent and moderate voters essential for winning competitive races.

Impact of January 6

The repercussions of January 6 continue to damage the party's standing and erode public trust.

Abortion Policy

Advocacy for stringent state-level abortion restrictions has proven unpopular with wide segments of the electorate, particularly moderates and suburban voters.

Uncertain Direction

The party continues to grapple with defining its identity, whether through continued alignment with Trump, a return to post-Trump conservatism, or adoption of new ideological directions.

Fundamental Challenge

While the Republican Party maintains a substantial and influential base, it has yet to build sufficient coalition breadth to secure consistent national victories.

Can the GOP Adapt to Modern Times Without Losing Its Conservative Identity?

It is important to clarify that modernization for the Republican Party does not necessarily entail adopting progressive values or abandoning its core conservative identity. The concept of modernization involves updating certain policies, strategies, or approaches to better address contemporary realities while still remaining rooted in the party's traditional principles. In other words, the process of modernization is distinct from a wholesale ideological shift toward progressivism.

It is a possible path, but it requires strategy, leadership, and a clear vision of what it means to be conservative in the 21st century.

Resistance to change is not technical but ideological.

The GOP has opted to reinforce its traditional conservative identity rather than adjust it to the country's cultural changes. This is not a miscalculation but a conscious decision.

The party has chosen to represent a specific segment of American society.

From a strategic perspective, the GOP does not see it as urgent to expand toward younger, urban, or more diverse sectors if its current base continues to guarantee electoral competitiveness. Therefore, the lack of adaptation does not stem from incapacity but from a preference for maintaining a clear and homogeneous identity.

Modernizing carries risks that the GOP prefers to avoid. Updating its platform to attract new voters could create internal tensions. These issues deeply divide its traditional base.

The GOP knows that a moderate shift could cause internal fractures, loss of rural support, and disengagement of its most loyal core. That is why, even though it can modernize, it does not want to pay the political cost of doing so. The U.S. political system, especially the Electoral College and the geographic distribution of votes, favors parties with strong support in rural and low-density states.

The GOP has understood this perfectly.

As long as its base is concentrated in key states in the South and Midwest, it can remain competitive without the need for deep transformation.

From this perspective, modernizing is not a necessity but an option that the party has chosen not to take, even if that means disconnecting from certain emerging sectors of American society.

How Does the GOP's Choice to Remain in the Past Affect the Country's Economic and Social Development?

The phrase "the GOP is not stuck in the past; it is choosing to remain there" suggests a strategic decision: to maintain a classic conservative identity rather than adapting to the social and economic changes of the 21st century.

Impact on the Modern Economy

Technological Competitiveness

Leading economists observe that the global economy increasingly depends on technological innovation, clean energy, automation, artificial intelligence, and digital infrastructure. When a political party is hesitant to endorse policies that support these sectors, the nation may experience diminished competitiveness relative to China, the European Union, or South Korea; delayed investments in emerging energy sources; reliance on outdated infrastructure; and limited advancement in workforce training for new industries.

While this does not indicate a complete rejection of technology by the GOP, its prioritization of traditional industries such as oil, conventional manufacturing, and coal may impede the transition toward higher-growth sectors.

Labor and Education

A thriving modern economy requires accessible higher education, technical training, and labor mobility. Emphasizing preservation of legacy industries over preparing the workforce for future demands can result in reduced productivity, stagnant wage growth, and the migration of skilled talent to states with more progressive educational policies.

Social Impact

Disconnect with Younger Generations

Emerging generations prioritize values including diversity, climate change, civil rights, the digital economy, and mental health. Failure to evolve messaging risks diminishing relevance among younger cohorts, exacerbating generational divisions, and constraining efforts to build national consensus.

Cultural Tensions

According to various analysts, rigid positions on social issues may contribute to increased polarization, hinder legislative negotiation, generate conflict between states with differing ideologies, and obstruct vital reforms in areas such as immigration, healthcare, and education. The inability to adapt affects not only the GOP but the broader political system's capacity to address contemporary challenges.

Institutional Impact

Legislative Standstill

Adherence to traditional perspectives without pursuing compromise complicates budget approvals, legal modernization, regulatory updates, and crisis response, directly influencing both economic and social progress.

Loss of International Competitiveness

Other nations continue to invest in advanced education, renew infrastructure, promote clean energy, and attract global expertise. Should domestic policy remain focused on prior debates, the United States faces the risk of lagging behind internationally.

Environmental and Economic Risks

Resistance to adopting modern environmental policies may result in increased vulnerability to natural disasters, higher public health expenditures, reduced competitiveness in renewable energy markets, and sustained reliance on fossil fuels, negatively impacting both economic performance and quality of life.

All of these scenarios have occurred, as it has been established that several harms are caused to the country when the GOP does not update its conservative policies to the 21st century. Updating is necessary to reduce the gap that exists between American society and the GOP in order to govern American society satisfactorily.

Summary

The American Democratic System Under Strain: Structural, Social, and Institutional Challenges in the 21st Century

The United States has long presented itself as a global model of democratic governance, constitutional stability, and political pluralism. Yet in the 21st century, the American democratic system faces a convergence of pressures that threaten its resilience and legitimacy. These pressures, including extreme polarization, weakening democratic institutions, money-driven politics, misinformation, persistent inequality, and widespread public distrust, do not operate independently. Instead, they interact in mutually reinforcing ways that undermine the foundations of democratic governance. Understanding this crisis requires examining each factor individually and then recognizing the systemic feedback loops that bind them together.

Extreme Polarization: From Ideological Disagreement to Identity Conflict

Political polarization in the United States has intensified to levels unseen in the modern era. While ideological differences have always existed, today's polarization is increasingly affective, rooted in emotion, identity, and social division rather than policy disagreement. Research from the Pew Research Center (2020) shows that Democrats and Republicans now view each other not merely as political opponents but as threats to the nation's well-being. Political scientist Lilliana Mason (2018) argues that partisan identity has fused with racial, religious, and cultural identities, creating "mega-identities" that heighten hostility and reduce the willingness to compromise.

This identity-based polarization has profound consequences. It transforms political competition into a zero-sum struggle, delegitimizes opposing viewpoints, and encourages citizens to interpret facts through partisan lenses. As a result, democratic norms such as tolerance, negotiation, and mutual respect erode. When political identity becomes a marker of moral worth, democratic deliberation becomes nearly impossible.

Weakening Democratic Institutions: Erosion from Within

Polarization contributes directly to the weakening of democratic institutions. Democracies depend not only on formal rules but also on informal norms, including restraint, respect for outcomes, and acceptance of institutional legitimacy. Levitsky and Ziblatt (2018) argue that modern democracies often fail not through violent coups but through gradual erosion, as political actors undermine norms and weaponize institutions for partisan gain.

In the United States, this erosion is visible in several areas:

- Congressional dysfunction, where gridlock has become routine.
- Judicial politicization, with courts increasingly perceived as partisan actors.
- Election administration disputes, where basic procedures are contested along party lines.
- Executive overreach, as presidents of both parties expand unilateral authority.

When institutions lose their perceived neutrality, citizens lose faith in their ability to act as fair arbiters. This delegitimization accelerates polarization and further weakens institutional stability.

Money-Driven Politics: Inequality of Influence

The influence of money in American politics has grown dramatically, especially after the Supreme Court's *Citizens United v. FEC* (2010) decision, which expanded the ability of corporations and outside groups to spend unlimited funds on political advocacy. According to the Center for Responsive Politics (2021), the 2020 election cycle was the most expensive in U.S. history, exceeding $14 billion in total spending.

This financial arms race distorts democratic representation. Wealthy donors, corporations, and interest groups gain disproportionate access to policymakers, while ordinary citizens struggle to make their voices heard. Political scientist Larry Bartels (2008) demonstrates that elected officials are significantly more responsive to the preferences of affluent constituents than to those of middle- or lower-income voters. When political influence correlates with wealth, the principle of political equality, central to democratic theory, is fundamentally compromised.

Misinformation: Fragmented Realities and Democratic Breakdown

The digital revolution has transformed the information landscape, enabling unprecedented access to information but also facilitating the rapid spread of misinformation. Social media platforms amplify emotionally charged content, regardless of accuracy. A landmark study by Vosoughi, Roy, and Aral (2018) found that false news spreads significantly faster and more widely than factual information on Twitter, largely because it is more novel and emotionally engaging.

This fragmentation of the information ecosystem undermines democracy in several ways:

- Citizens no longer share a common set of facts.
- Conspiracy theories gain traction and influence political behavior.
- Trust in journalism, science, and expertise declines.
- Elections become vulnerable to manipulation by domestic and foreign actors.

Without a shared reality, democratic deliberation collapses. Misinformation fuels polarization, delegitimizes institutions, and deepens public distrust.

Inequality: Economic and Social Divides as Democratic Fault Lines

Economic inequality in the United States has reached levels comparable to the early 20th century. According to the U.S. Census Bureau (2022), income inequality has steadily increased over the past five decades. Inequality affects democracy in multiple ways:

- It reduces social mobility and economic opportunity.
- It creates political resentment among marginalized groups.
- It concentrates political influence among the wealthy.
- It undermines the belief that democratic institutions serve all citizens equally.

Economist Joseph Stiglitz (2012) argues that inequality is not merely an economic issue but a political one: it distorts representation, weakens social cohesion, and erodes trust in government. When citizens feel excluded from economic prosperity, they are more likely to disengage from democratic participation or support anti-establishment movements.

Public Distrust: The Crisis of Legitimacy

All these pressures culminate in a profound crisis of public trust. Surveys show that trust in government is near historic lows, with only about 20% of Americans expressing confidence that the federal government will do what is right most of the time (Pew Research Center, 2022). Trust in Congress, the media, and other institutions is similarly low.

Distrust is both a symptom and a driver of democratic decline. When citizens distrust institutions, they are less likely to participate in elections, follow laws, or accept political outcomes. This creates a feedback loop: weakened institutions produce distrust, and distrust further weakens institutions.

Conclusion: A Self-Reinforcing Cycle That Demands Democratic Renewal

The American democratic system is strained by a constellation of forces, including polarization, institutional erosion, money-driven politics, misinformation, inequality, and distrust, that reinforce one another in a destabilizing cycle. Addressing these challenges requires more than policy adjustments; it demands a renewal of democratic norms, a commitment to institutional integrity, and a collective effort to rebuild trust. The resilience of American democracy has been tested before, but the current crisis is unique in its complexity and interconnectedness. Its future will depend on whether citizens and leaders can confront these pressures with honesty, courage, and a renewed dedication to democratic principles.

References

APA 7th Edition

Bartels, L. (2008). *Unequal democracy: The political economy of the new gilded age.* Princeton University Press.

Center for Responsive Politics. (2021). *Cost of election 2020.* OpenSecrets.

Levitsky, S., & Ziblatt, D. (2018). *How democracies die.* Crown.

Mason, L. (2018). *Uncivil agreement: How politics became our identity.* University of Chicago Press.

Pew Research Center. (2020). *Political polarization in the American public.*

Pew Research Center. (2022). *Public trust in government: 1958–2022.*

Stiglitz, J. (2012). *The price of inequality.* W. W. Norton & Company.

U.S. Census Bureau. (2022). *Income and poverty in the United States.*

Vosoughi, S., Roy, D., & Aral, S. (2018). The spread of true and false news online. *Science, 359*(6380), 1146–1151.